FHIR DATA
SOLUTIONS

WITH AZURE FHIR SERVER, AZURE API FOR FHIR & AZURE HEALTH DATA SERVICES

INCLUDES END-TO-END DESIGN
PHI DATA LAKE FOR EHR, OMICS, IMAGING, IOMT, WEARABLES & BUSINESS DATA

A complete guide to the hl7 history- data standards –
PHI echo system analysis with solutions

BY AJIT DASH

Dedicated

to

Almighty

iv

Table of Contents

PREFACE

Welcome to the preface of this book on revolutionizing the health care industry through digitization and the adoption of Health Level Seven International (HL7) data standards, specifically focusing on Fast Healthcare Interoperability Resources (FHIR) and Azure Health Data Services (AHDS). In this book, we will explore the transformative potential of these technologies and their applications in modern healthcare systems.

The health care industry is undergoing a significant revolution driven by digital transformation. The integration of technology and data standards has the power to enhance patient care, improve operational efficiency, and enable better collaboration among health care providers. With the increasing adoption of FHIR and AHDS, health care organizations can unlock the true potential of their data and facilitate interoperability across different systems.

In Chapter 1, we will delve into the introduction, discussing the health care industry revolution, digitization, and the challenges faced by modern health care systems. We will also explore government regulations and the concept of Meaningful Use.

Chapter 2 will focus on FHIR standards, their adoption, and the advantages they offer in promoting interoperability. We will explore an example of a FHIR resource, specifically the Patient resource, to illustrate its practical application.

Moving on to Chapter 3, we will dive into the FHIR infrastructure and services, including the FHIR Server for Azure and Azure API for FHIR. We will also explore how Azure services like Data Lake and Azure Databricks can be leveraged in conjunction with FHIR for managing Protected Health Information (PHI).

Chapter 4 will introduce you to Azure Health Data Services (AHDS), providing an overview of its components such as Azure API for FHIR and DICOM

(Digital Imaging and Communications in Medicine). We will explore the features and applications of DICOM and highlight the potential of MedTech in real-time data processing using Internet of Medical Things (IoMT) technologies.

In Chapter 5, we will take a deeper dive into PHI Data Lake using AHDS. We will explore the data flow within the PHI Data Lake and present a reference architecture for building a secure and scalable PHI Data Lake infrastructure.

Finally, Chapter 6 will conclude our exploration, summarizing the key insights and findings. We will also provide references for further reading and a bibliography of the sources used throughout this book.

This book aims to serve professionals and enthusiasts in the health care industry who are eager to explore the potential of FHIR, AHDS, and related technologies. It is designed to provide practical knowledge, insights, and reference materials to empower readers in their digital transformation journey.

I hope you find this book insightful, informative, and valuable in your pursuit of revolutionizing health care through digitization and the adoption of FHIR and AHDS.

Wishing you an enriching reading experience.

Author -Ajit Dash

WHOM IS THIS BOOK FOR?

This book is intended for professionals and enthusiasts in the health care industry who are eager to explore the potential of revolutionizing health care through digitization and the adoption of Fast Healthcare Interoperability Resources (FHIR) and Azure Health Data Services (AHDS). It caters to individuals who are interested in understanding the transformative impact of these technologies and their applications in modern health care systems.

Specifically, this book targets:

1. Health care professionals: Doctors, nurses, medical practitioners, and administrators who want to stay updated on the latest advancements in health care technology and how it can enhance patient care and operational efficiency.

2. Health IT professionals: Professionals working in the field of health information technology, electronic health records, health informatics, and data management who seek practical knowledge and insights into FHIR and AHDS for interoperability and data exchange.

3. Health care executives and decision-makers: Leaders and decision-makers in health care organizations who want to explore the potential of FHIR and AHDS to drive digital transformation initiatives and improve overall organizational efficiency.

4. Researchers and academicians: Scholars, researchers, and students in the field of health care, health informatics, and health data management who wish to deepen their understanding of FHIR, AHDS, and their applications in health care research and analysis.

5. Technology enthusiasts: Individuals with a keen interest in emerging technologies and their impact on the health care industry who want to gain practical knowledge and insights into FHIR and AHDS.

Regardless of your specific background or role within the health care industry, this book aims to provide valuable insights, practical examples, and reference materials to empower you in your journey of leveraging FHIR and AHDS for digital transformation and revolutionizing health care.

xiv

CHAPTER 1

INTRODUCTION

Health Care Industry Revolution & Digitization:

The healthcare industry revolution has put a great deal of emphasis on data in order to improve patient outcomes in an advanced manner. In order to maximize the effectiveness of utilizing EHR (Electronic Health Records) records, it is crucial to ensure they are formatted in the right way. This type of system will ensure that there is interoperability across all parts of the healthcare ecosystem. This is due to the way U.S. healthcare is organized in the country and how it functions.

Digitization/Computer revolutions and corporation shifts to computers resulted in many manual processes being eliminated, and among them, the healthcare industry was revolutionized as well by converting all manual record handling of patient medical records, clinical care information, payers & insurance companies, etc., into electronic systems (EHRs - Electronic Health Records). In order to provide quality care as quickly as possible, the emphasis was always on the efficient handling of patients and the interoperability of patient records. This was to meet the agile demands of patient information, which always includes vital information about the patient. This facilitates fast decision-making and prompts attention to cases as they arise.

Health Level Seven International (HL7) Data Standards[1]:

Hence, Health Level Seven International (HL7), which was founded in 1987 and is a not-for-profit organization with a vision of "To enable global health data interoperability by establishing standards that enable secure access and use of the right health

---

[1] https://www.hl7.org/about/index.cfm?ref=nav

data." and a mission of "Providing health data standards that enable secure access and use.".

In HL7, a framework was established for the support of secure messaging and document exchange between healthcare organizations. A key purpose of these standards is to facilitate the exchange, integration, sharing, and retrieval of electronic health information for use in clinical practice, management, delivery, and evaluation. Globally, it supports healthcare providers, government stakeholders, payers, pharmaceutical companies, vendors, and suppliers.

HL7 V2 was released in 1989 and has become one of the most widely implemented healthcare standards globally. The majority of U.S. medical organizations use HL7 today.

HL7 V2 facilitates communication between systems, such as electronic medical records (EMRs), health information systems, laboratory information systems, billing systems, etc. ASCII text is used in those messages. When a patient is admitted to a clinic, when a specialist submits a pharmacy request, and when a healthcare provider charges a patient, frameworks communicate information between themselves. This integration helps Healthcare organizations to avoid complex software interface development work by using HL7 V2 to communicate between various systems.

Challenges with Modern Healthcare Systems

As per the statistics, 88 % of healthcare organizations in USA adopted EHR systems[2]

Digitalization and technological growth have posed some significant challenges to modern healthcare systems.

1. **Interoperability:** The ability to capture and annotate health data from traditional as well as emerging systems

---

[2] https://dashboard.healthit.gov/quickstats/pages/physician-ehr-adoption-trends.php

2. **Security:** Maintain the security and privacy of all patients' personal medical information (PHI).

3. **Compliance:** Implement advanced analytics and machine learning technology that is compliant with laws and regulations relating to health data

4. **Missing medical records[3]:** An inpatient study found that 18% of medical errors which led to adverse drug events could be traced back to missing data in the patient's medical record as part of their responsibility as a primary care provider (PCP) in 117 organizations. PCPs coordinate care with 229 other physicians in 117 organizations as part of providing care for their patients.

5. **Digital Adoption:** In the medical industry, digital devices such as wearables, IoMTs (Internet of Medical Things) and monitors are

---

[3] **JMIRPublications** Validation and Testing of Fast Healthcare Interoperability Resources Standards Compliance: Data Analysis by Jason Walonoski1, MS ; Robert Scanlon1, MS ; Conor Dowling1 ; Mario Hyland2 ; Richard Ettema2, BS ; Steven Posnack3, MS, MHS - https://medinform.jmir.org/2018/4/e10870/

widely adopted to receive vital information instantly. This is also becoming a challenge.

Government Regulation & Meaning Full Use

A key feature of Health Information Technology for Economic and Clinical Health (HITECH) is Meaningful Use (MU), which is part of the American Recovery and Reinvestment Act (ARRA), passed by Congress in 2009 and signed by President Obama. MU promotes meaningful, coordinated, and integrated use of EHRs.[4]

As a means of complying with government regulations and overcoming all the challenges created by the growth of data, the HL7 organization developed a new standard called HL7 FHIR. With the introduction of new government incentives and Meaningful Use requirements, along with HL7 FHIR standards and open-source technology, it is now possible to create a truly integrated ecosystem for

---

[4] https://www.cms.gov/newsroom/fact-sheets/2016-medicare-electronic-health-record-ehr-incentive-programpayment-adjustment-fact-sheet-critical#:~:text=The%20American%20Recovery%20and%20Reinvestment,Health%20Record%20Technology%20(CEHRT).

Health Information Exchange (HIE) that is driven by all of these factors.

CHAPTER 2

FHIR STANDARDS

FHIR Standards & Adoption

F HIR, or Fast Healthcare Interoperability Resources (hl7.org/fhir), is a next-generation standard developed by HL7 and introduced in 2014[5]. The proposed standard is an essential alternative to HL7 V2 and V3. Healthcare institutions quickly adopted FHIR, including Common Well Health Alliance and SMART (Substitutable Medical Applications, Reusable Technologies). The primary aim of FHIR is to standardize access to meaningful use data that can be found in EHRs (Electronic Health Records) and other systems of record product lines. This can be achieved by merging key features from

---

[5] Index - FHIR v1.0.2 (hl7.org)

HL7's v2, v3, and Clinical Document Architecture (CDA) product lines standards for standardizing Meaningful Use data access. A key feature of FHIR is its leveraging of the latest web standards such as Restful web services, open web technologies, XML and JSON data format, for data exchange/communication among systems and its emphasis on low-cost implementation throughout its deployment process.

In FHIR solutions, components called "Resources" are combined into a solution. It is possible to combine these resources into working systems that solve clinical and administrative problems in real-world settings at a fraction of the cost of alternatives that are currently available. Various scenarios can benefit from FHIR through multiple data-sharing options, for example, messaging (like HL7 V2), documents (like CDA), and a RESTful API for devices. Leveraging Restful APIs enhances communication for mobile apps, Mobile devices, IoMTs (Internet of Medical Things), wearables, cloud communications, electronic health records (EHRs) data sharing, and server communication among large institutional healthcare providers.

Details about the FHIR process and the modules such as Clinical, Diagnostic, Medications, Workflow & Financials available in hl7.org/fhir)[6]

Advantages of FHIR[7]

Implementation: Implementation is fast and easy

Standards: XML, JSON, HTTP, OAuth, and other Web standards

Data Access: A RESTful architecture, a seamless exchange of documents or messages, and a service-based architecture are all supported. Concise and easily understood specifications.

Legacy: A development path from HL7 Version 2 to CDA: standards can co-exist and work together

Easy: Serialization format (human-readable) that developers can use easily

---

[6] http://hl7.org/fhir/?utm_referrer=https%3A%2F%2Fwww.hl7.org%2F
[7] http://hl7.org/fhir/summary.html

Adoption: Using Profiles, Extensions, Terminologies, and more, base resources can be adapted as needed for local requirements, which occurs quite often. Also, there are no restrictions on the use of the specification

More About CDA, C-CDA[8]

Clinical Document Architecture (CDA) documents are XML documents. C-CDA are a set of guidelines/templates for specific document types such as Continuity of Care Document (CCD), Discharge Summary, etc.

Example of a Resources: Patient

This image shows a simple Resource and the Human Readable HTML format

---

[8] https://github.com/HL7/C-CDA-Examples

```xml
<Patient xmlns="http://hl7.org/fhir">
  <id value="glossy"/>
  <meta>
    <lastUpdated value="2014-11-13T11:41:00+11:00"/>
  </meta>
  <text>
    <status value="generated"/>
    <div xmlns="http://www.w3.org/1999/xhtml">
      <p>Henry Levin the 7th</p>
      <p>MRN: 123456. Male, 24-Sept 1932</p>
    </div>
  </text>
  <extension url="http://example.org/StructureDefinition/trials">
    <valueCode value="renal"/>
  </extension>
  <identifier>
    <use value="usual"/>
    <type>
      <coding>
        <system value="http://hl7.org/fhir/v2/0203"/>
        <code value="MR"/>
      </coding>
    </type>
    <system value="http://www.goodhealth.org/identifiers/mrn"/>
    <value value="123456"/>
  </identifier>
  <active value="true"/>
  <name>
    <family value="Levin"/>
    <given value="Henry"/>
    <suffix value="The 7th"/>
  </name>
  <gender value="male"/>
  <birthDate value="1932-09-24"/>
  <careProvider>
    <reference value="Organization/2"/>
    <display value="Good Health Clinic"/>
  </careProvider>
</Patient>
```

Resource Identity & Metadata

Human Readable Summary

Extension with URL to definition

Standard Data:
• MRN
• Name
• Gender
• Birth Date
• Provider

Reference: http://hl7.org/fhir/summary.html#2.17.3

12

CHAPTER 3

FHIR INFRASTRUCTURE

FHIR Infrastructure and Services

Industrial clouds have made it possible for cloud providers to provide FHIR services and infrastructure. In this article, I will describe the FHIR infrastructure and services available in Microsoft Azure.

1. **FHIR Server for Azure**

2. **Azure API for FHIR**

3. **Azure Health Data Services**

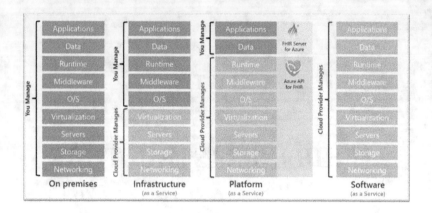

On premises	Infrastructure (as a Service)	Platform (as a Service)	Software (as a Service)

FHIR Server for Azure

It is recommended that developers use the open-source FHIR Server for Azure if customizing a FHIR server requires admin access to underlying services (e.g., access to databases without going through the FHIR API).[9]

100 % Open source & Full control

Deployed in Azure Subscription

Available in GitHub

Built managed and maintained by Microsoft.

Designed for compliance management.

FHIR Server for Azure

Data Lake (PHI) using FHIR Server for Azure & Synapse

1 Source EMR records Converted to FHIR Standards using HL7 Converter

2 FHIR Bundle load using HL7 bulk loading function to the FHIR Server for Azure

3 Data from FHIR Server pulled using Synapse pipeline or directly to the ADLS using APIs

4 Synapse read those data from ADLS for downstream consumptions

5 Data in the Databricks available for downstream consumptions such as Cognitive , ML ,Bot and Report

Synapse   Azure Databricks

6 Synapse can be replaced by Databricks

Synapse Pipeline   ADF

7 Instead Synapse Pipeline can be replaced with ADF or other data ingestion tool /APIs

Azure API for FHIR

The FHIR service provides developers with a ready-to-use FHIR API that includes a provisioned database backend (data is only accessible through the API, not directly from the database).[10]

Managed FHIR server offered as a PaaS in Azure

Provisioned easily through Azure portal.

Meets regulatory compliance for PHI (Protected Healthcare Information)

Azure API for FHIR

Data Lake (PHI) using Azure API for FHIR & Azure Databricks

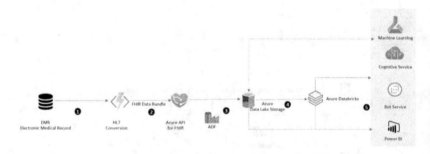

1. Source EMR records Converted to FHIR Standards using HL7 Converter

2. FHIR Bundle load using HL7 bulk loading function to the Azure API for FHIR

3. Data from Azure API for FHIR pulled / pushed using ADF or directly to the ADLS

4. Databricks read those data from ADLS (DB Spark Framework) for downstream consumptions

5. Data in the Databricks available for downstream consumptions such as Cognitive , ML ,Bot and Report

Azure Databricks   Synapse

6. Databricks can be replaced by Synapse

ADF   Synapse Pipeline

7. ADF can be replaced with Synapse Pipeline or other data ingestion tool /APIs

CHAPTER 4

AZURE HEALTH DATA SERVICES (AHDS)

Azure Health Data Services:

Azure Health Data Services (AHDS) is a set of managed API services based on open standards and frameworks to enable workflows to improve healthcare. AHDS platform is a platform as a service (PaaS). Besides FHIR, Azure Health Data Services offers managed services for other types of health data, such as the DICOM (Digital Imaging and Communications in Medicine) service for medical imaging data and the MedTech service for medical IoMT (Internet of Medical Things) data, which are part of the Azure Health Data Services portfolio. In an Azure Health Data Services workspace, all services

(FHIR service, DICOM service, and MedTech service) can be connected and administered.

- FHIR API endpoint for accessing and storing FHIR data that is enterprise-grade.

- Cloud-based protection of protected health information (PHI) HIPAA, HITRUST

- Mobile and web clients for SMART on FHIR

- Role-Based Access Control (RBAC) in Azure Active Directory

- The FHIR audit log tracks access, creation, and modification events

Azure API for FHIR managed PaSS
Enterprise-grade FHIR API for storage and data access
SMART on FHIR for mobile and web clients
PHI data compliance with HIPPA

Azure Health Data Services Secured Platform for PHI Data
Consumes multiple data format using FHIR API Service, DIACOM (medical imaging data) & MedTech (medical IoT, wearable, monitor etc. data)

DICOM (Digital Imaging and Communications in Medicine)
It is used for the ingest and persist Image data.
Enables PHI data ingestion with PHI compliance.

MedTech service is an integrated service with AHDS.
MedTech service is used for processing IoTM, Monitors, and Wearable devices.

1. Azure API for FHIR

As discussed in section #2 above. It's an integrated service of the AHDS package.

2. DICOM (Digital Imaging and Communications in Medicine) [11]

DICOM is the primary medical imaging standard in healthcare industry that can be used to transmit, store, retrieve, print, process, and display medical images.

---

[11] https://learn.microsoft.com/en-us/azure/healthcare-apis/dicom/dicom-services-overview

AHDS DICOM is a managed service that ingests and persists DICOM objects at a rate of multiple thousand images per second. Imaging data can be communicated and transmitted to DICOM web-enabled systems and applications via DICOM web's standard APIs, such as Store (STOW-RS), Search (QIDO-RS), and Retrieve (WADO-RS). One can upload PHI data to the DICOM service and exchange it securely as a PaaS offering in the cloud.

DICOM Features[12] :

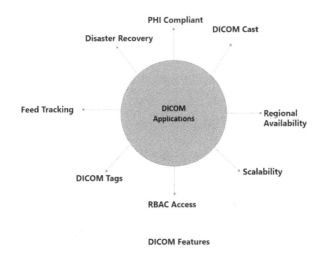

DICOM Features

---

[12] https://learn.microsoft.com/en-us/azure/healthcare-apis/dicom/dicom-services-overview

- **PHI Compliant:** PHI data is protected and secured against all kinds of threats and disasters. Multiple region failover protection is provided, and data protection is isolated as per the API instances.

- **DICOMcast:** With DICOMcast, DICOM metadata can be injected into a FHIR service, or FHIR server, in order to provide a single source of truth for both clinical data and imaging metadata. This feature is available on demand.

- **Region availability:** multi-region failover protection to assure data availability.

- **Scalability:** DICOM service scales to meet the needs of multiple regions, global and local requirements, and load requirements

- **Role-based Access (RBAC):** DICOM provides RBAC functionality, which enables data to be accessed more efficiently while ensuring data security.

- **DICOM Tags:** The information contained in a DICOM file, known as a data set, is encoded in a series of key-value associative arrays that describe the medical information contained within it. There can be a hierarchy of values (called a sequence), similar to an XML or JSON file. In DICOM, each key is assigned a DICOM tag.

- **Feed Change Tracking:** All the services to the DICOM feed can be tracked and viewed. Applications can read these logs independently, simultaneously, and at their own pace.

Application of DICOM:

Patients' diagnosis records, past medical history, current medication, clinical information, and other supplementary information, such as image meta-data, are required to establish a diagnosis for treatment. In order to deliver an effective treatment plan, data from various sources must be presented in a particular format. As part of the DICOM service, imaging data can be securely stored in Azure, in the same subscription as EHRs and IoT data.

Increasingly critical for clinical data, FHIR offers extensibility to support integrating other types of data directly or through references, making it a necessary standard. The DICOM service enables organizations to store imaging data in FHIR and to execute queries that span clinical and imaging data.

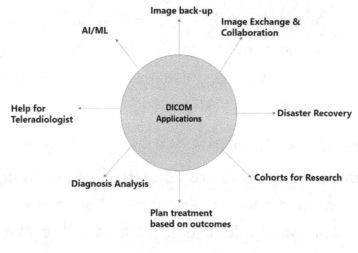

DICOM Services Applications

These are some examples of DICOM services available:

1. Image backup

Images from various imaging centers such as a research institution, clinic, imaging center, veterinary clinic, pathology institution, retailer, or any other team or organization. DICOM can back up images and provide unlimited storage and access to images. Furthermore, it is validated for PHI compliance, so there is no need to de-identify patient data.

2. Image exchange & Collaboration

Whether you want to share one image, a subset of images in your storage, or the entire image library, you can do so instantly with or without EHR data

3. Disaster Recovery

It provides high availability.

4. Cohort for research

In conjunction with EHR, DICOM provides reference data that assists in determining the diagnosis that has been given to the patient. For example, give me the last two years' recommendations, CT scan, MRI images with medication recommendation of any patient above age 60 who has Paraganglioma.

5. Plan treatment

If a physician is presented with a patient's diagnosis, he or she can quickly identify patient outcomes and treatment plans for past patients with a similar diagnosis, even if the imaging data have already been gathered.

6. Diagnosis Analysis

Many radiologists, especially those that work with teleradiology, are not equipped with complete access to the patient's medical history as well as imaging studies related to the patient. In order to provide this data easily, the FHIR integration could also allow radiologists outside the organizations' local network to access it.

7. Help for Teleradiologist

If a radiologist makes a recommendation, he or she should have access to the hospital's clinical data. This is not always the case for teleradiologists. Since they don't have access to patient data after the initial read, they are often unable to close the feedback loop. It is impossible for them to improve their skills without access to clinical results. With the integration of FHIR standards and DICOM, these gaps can easily be filled.

8. AI/ML

The performance of machine learning models is best enhanced by real-world feedback. Models provided by third parties rarely receive the feedback they need to improve. In the case of brain surgery, doctors use a combination of machine models and human experts."Physicians rarely provide feedback on the accuracy of the recommendations. The only customer and doctor feedback available to all is if there's a major issue with the recommendations. Like with teleradiology feedback, organizations can integrate FHIR into their model retraining pipeline to obtain feedback.

Example for the Cohort for Research:

Problem Statement:

The patient is suffering from Paraganglioma, a rare form of tumor that causes buzzing in the ears.

Services:

The AHDS DICOM service is used for recommendations and suggestions. In conjunction with EHR data, DICOM is used to analyze image metadata.

Reference Data:

The system provides the previous two years' recommendations, CT scan, and MRI of a patient below 45 with a paraganglioma. This information helps the doctor develop a treatment plan.

With DICOMcast, DICOM metadata can be injected into an FHIR service or FHIR server. This will provide a single source of truth for both clinical data and imaging metadata. Clinical information includes medThis feature is available on demand.

Security:

All the data/metadata/images are PHI Compliant

Example for the Cohort for Research

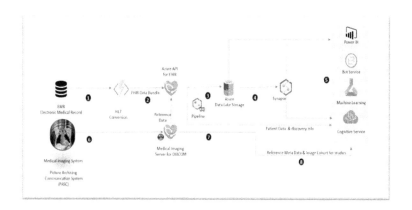

Synapse   Azure Databricks

9 Synapse can be replaced by Azure Databricks

Synapse Pipeline   ADF

Synapse Pipeline can be replaced with ADF or other data ingestion tool /APIs

1. Source EMR records Converted to FHIR Standards using HL7 Converter

2. FHIR Bundle load using HL7 bulk loading function to the Azure API for FHIR

3. Data from Azure API for FHIR pulled / pushed using ADF or directly to the ADLS

4. Databricks read those data from ADLS (DB Spark Framework) for downstream consumptions

5. Data in the Databricks available for downstream consumptions such as Cognitive , ML ,Bot and Data

6. Medical Imaging data from PASC system available for processing

7. Medical Imaging Server for DIACOM processed the data and make it available for analysis

8. Reference data and EMR data readily available for the further analysis

3. MedTech

MedTech service is a part of the services provided by Azure Health Data Services (AHDS). It is a platform as a service (PaaS). It collects information from a wide range of medical devices and converts it into consumable standard data formats Fast Healthcare Interoperability Resources (FHIR®).

In order to provide customers with better services, MedTech offers the ability to unify various data sources, each having its own data format, into a unified FHIR format.

MedTech uses a wide range of devices to consume information, including wearables (watches, medical device sensors, etc.), health care devices, ambulance medical sensors, critical care sensors, and so on. Each of these devices sends a different kind of signal, and these signals are converted to a unified format (FHIR) using MedTech to be processed in real-time, near real-time, or batch modes, depending on whether it is sent in real-time, near real-time, or batch mode.

This enables the data processing and downstream data analysis needed for machine learning and data science or reporting. In the absence of unified data formats, it is very challenging to analyze device data. From consumption to unification, MedTech keeps it simple, including further information retrieval downstream. As a result, this facilitates medical professionals in taking care of crucial decisions.

Data Processing in MedTech Real Time Wearable, Ambulance Sensors (Using IoMT) [13]

1. **Source Ingest:** Hight speed source data first comes to IOT Hub then it goes to Event Hub(temporarily hold the information before process it ac) . IOT Hub is uses because it provides the acknowledgement to the received data from device.

2. **MedTech Process:**

   a. Ingest- Data from the event hub is asynchronously loaded by the MedTech service.

   b. Cleansed – Received data cleansed for any anomaly.

---

[13] https://learn.microsoft.com/en-us/azure/healthcare-apis/iot/overview

c. Normalized - The MedTech service uses device mapping to streamline and convert ingested data into a normalized schema.

d. Group - Normalized data is grouped by parameters for the next stage of processing. There are four parameters: device ID, measurement type, time period, and correlation ID.

3. **Transform** - After the normalized data is grouped, it is transformed using FHIR destination mapping templates and is ready for use as an observation resource.

4. **Persist** - Once the transformation is complete, the new data is sent to FHIR service and persisted.

5. **Access for FHIR** – Data is available in FHIR standard

6. **Down Stream Consumption:** Standard FHIR data can be access using API for downstream

analysis /consumptions (to storage / report / ML etc.)

Application:

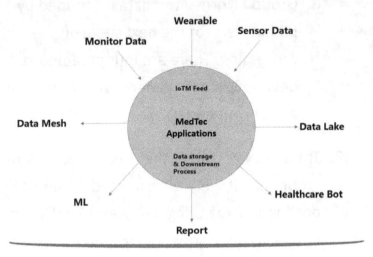

Used by Physician team, clinician, laboratory, or research facility

MedTec Features

Data from MedTec can be processed further in Data Lake, Data Mesh, ML, health care reports, and health care suggestions using BOT. This information can be very useful to **physicians, clinicians, laboratories, and research facilities.**

CHAPTER 5

PHI DATA LAKE USING AHDS

PHI Data Lake Using Azure Health Data Services

PHI Data Lake Data Flow

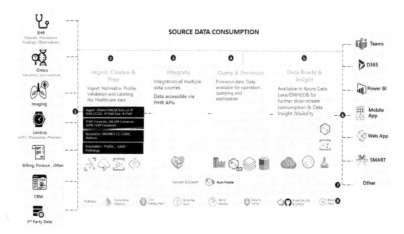

Horizonal View

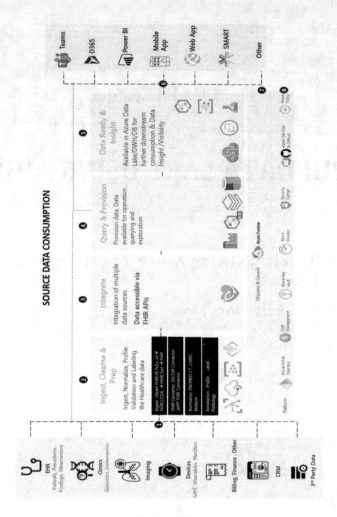

Vertical View

PHI Data Lake Data Flow

1. **Source data** from various sources such as PHI CRM data, IoMT ,Images Meta Data are available

2. **Ingested** data as raw format, cleansed and normalized with healthcare standards (FHIR)

3. **Data from multiple data sources** after convert to the standard **integrated** for value creation as required by the final deliverables

4. **Data ready for query and exploration** as required for the final deliverables

5. Data is ready for downstream consumption to a DWH , Data Lake ,DB & File format etc.

6. Data is ready for downstream consumptions prepared for the visibility layer – report , mobile app , web app etc.

7. Data governance layer manage and maintain the data quality and data integrity

8. Platform governance through Azure services for the security , activity, cost mgmt., in the Azure platform and for any vulnerability detection ex : Key Vault , Monitor ,Devops ,Cost Advisor etc.

PHI Data Lake Reference Architecture

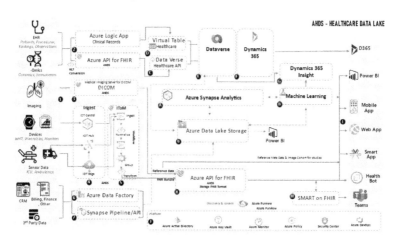

Horizonal View

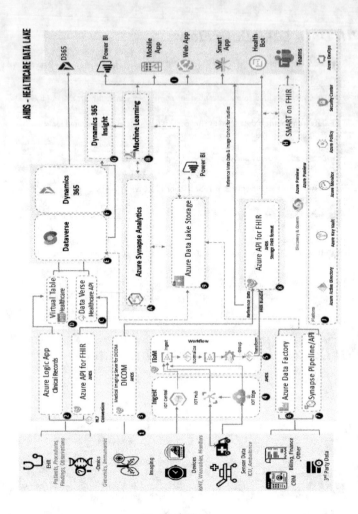

Vertical View

① Source information –different types Sensor, Images , Clinical & CRM others ..

② Azure Logic App collect the source data (clinical records) and pass to the virtual table
HL7 Converts the source data to FHIR standard using Azure API for FHIR (AHDS Service) .

③ Digital Imaging and Communications in Medicine (DICOM) an AHDS service for image processing

④ Ingest source data either by IOT Central ,IOT Hub directly or IOT Hub with IOT Edge capabilities

IOT Central : It centralize device data

IOT Hub transmits information to IOT Central from all devices connected to it. It is a PaaS service that allows bidirectional communication between a device and an IOT application .Provides device authentication by acknowledgement to the connected device, build in device management and provision

IOT Edge : It provides the computing capabilities & pass the device data to IOT Hub .This helps the devices with limited storage and computing capability.

⑤ Ingest data from IOT hub,IOT Central and IOT Edge processed further using the workflow which is consists of three steps ingest , normalize and group

Ingest : Event Hub : Data ingested from IOT hub, IOT Central and IOT Edge to event hub fully managed service and have capability to process millions of events real time and scalable as needed
Normalized : Data being normalized with the associated relationship (with key value pair /timeseries) data using EventHub and serverless function

Group : Similar data pairs and grouped using the Azure stream analytics service a serverless service with customer code and machine learning capabilities

All transformed data readily available as FHIR Bundle and consumed by
Azure API for FHIR

6 7 Data from other application such as CRM, Finance or 3rd party data processed either by the Azure Data Factory/Synapse Pipeline /API

8 Azure API for FHIR an AHDS service

9 All the data after process stored in the Azure Data Lake Storage (ADLS)

A Data in Azure Data Lake Storage processed further using Azure Synapse Analytics (SQL, Spark) it has database schema templets available

B Data from Azure Data Lake Storage (ADLS) available for Machine learning /training the ML Model

C Dataverse API data collects the FHIR standard patient observation , Genomics etc. .data and store in the Dataverse (storage)

D Logic App service collects the FHIR standard patient observation , Genomics etc. .data and store in the Dataverse (storage)

E Dataverse stores the data in table format row & column and part of Dynamic365 application

F Dynamic 365 is an intelligence application it has functionality of combination of CRM and ERP .It can be easily customized as per the business requirement and stores the data in inbuilt db Dataverse

G It is real time customer data platform, and it provides comprehensive view of the source data . It built on the Azure platform and have capabilities of the Azure analytics and Azure machine learning capability

H Data available to Teams app using Smart on FHIR

I Processed source data available for the downstream consumption and visibility Power. Mobile App. ML , Health Care BOT .Smart app etc.

J Data Governance and Metadata Management accomplished by Azure Purview
Platform utilization and performance managed by Azure Services such as Azure Monitor, Azure Key Vault for Secrete Key management,Azure Policy , Azure Active Directory
Data Deployment accomplish by GitHub and DevOps

CHAPTER 6

CONCLUSION

I n conclusion, this book offers a comprehensive exploration of the revolution and digitization taking place in the healthcare industry, with a specific focus on the adoption of Health Level Seven International (HL7) data standards and Fast Healthcare Interoperability Resources (FHIR) infrastructure. Throughout the chapters, we have delved into various aspects of these topics, including the challenges faced by modern healthcare systems and the advantages of implementing FHIR standards.

Chapter 1 serves as an introduction, providing an overview of the health care industry revolution and the role of digitization. It also emphasizes the significance of government regulations and meaningful use in shaping the future of healthcare systems.

Chapter 2 focuses on FHIR standards and their adoption. It highlights the advantages of utilizing FHIR and offers an example of a resource, specifically the Patient resource, showcasing the practical implementation of FHIR.

Moving on to Chapter 3, we explore the FHIR infrastructure and services available. The chapter discusses the FHIR server for Azure and its role in creating a data lake for protected health information (PHI) using Azure Synapse. It also introduces the Azure API for FHIR and its integration with Azure Databricks for data processing.

Chapter 4 introduces Azure Health Data Services (AHDS), which encompasses various components such as Azure API for FHIR, DICOM (Digital Imaging and Communications in Medicine), and MedTech. The chapter explores the features and applications of DICOM and illustrates the use of MedTech in real-time data processing, leveraging wearable devices and ambulance sensors.

In Chapter 5, we delve into the creation of a PHI data lake using AHDS. The chapter presents the data flow within the PHI data lake and discusses the reference architecture for its implementation.

Finally, Chapter 6 serves as the conclusion of this book. It summarizes the key insights and findings presented throughout the chapters, emphasizing the importance of HL7 data standards, FHIR infrastructure, and AHDS in transforming the health care industry. It also invites readers to explore further resources and references provided in Chapter 7, 8, and 9 for additional reading and in-depth understanding.

In conclusion, this book aims to equip healthcare professionals, IT specialists, and individuals interested in the intersection of healthcare and technology with the knowledge and insights necessary to navigate the evolving landscape of digital health. By embracing the concepts and technologies explored in this book, we can strive towards a more connected, efficient, and patient-centric healthcare ecosystem.

Please note that this conclusion is a sample based solely on the table of contents provided, and the actual content of the book may differ.

CHAPTER 7

FURTHER READING

Further Reading:

1. Health Level Seven International (HL7). (n.d.). https://www.hl7.org/.

2. Office of the National Coordinator for Health Information Technology. (n.d.). Meaningful Use. https://www.healthit.gov/topic/meaningful-use.

3. HL7 FHIR. (n.d.). https://www.hl7.org/fhir/.

4. Microsoft Azure. (n.d.). https://azure.microsoft.com/.

5. Azure API for FHIR. (n.d.).
https://azure.microsoft.com/services/azure-api-for-fhir/.

6. DICOM Standard. (n.d.).
https://www.dicomstandard.org/.

7. MedTech Europe. (n.d.).
https://www.medtecheurope.org/.

8. Internet of Medical Things (IoMT). (n.d.).
https://www.himss.org/resources/iot-and-digital-transformation-healthcare.

9. Azure Data Lake Storage. (n.d.).
https://azure.microsoft.com/services/storage/data-lake-storage/.

10. Azure Databricks. (n.d.).
https://azure.microsoft.com/services/databricks/.

11. Azure Synapse Analytics. (n.d.).
https://azure.microsoft.com/services/synapse-analytics/.

12. HealthIT.gov. (n.d.). https://www.healthit.gov/.

CHAPTER 8

ABOUT AUTHOR

Ajit Dash is a seasoned professional with over 24 years of experience in data and analytics. He has held various roles, including Senior Director of Data, Cloud Advisor, Solution Architect, and Data Scientist Lead. Ajit specializes in providing enterprise and cross-platform integration solutions to corporations across industries such as Telecommunication, Biotech, Finance, Banking, Media, Aerospace, Insurance, and Technology.

Ajit's expertise includes AI, Generative AI, Enterprise Solution Architecture, Cloud Advisory, Data Lake, Big Data, Data Science, Data Warehousing, Database Management, and BI Reporting. He has collaborated with clients like Fox, Oshkosh, Otis, Travelers, Apple, Qualcomm, IBM, and LPL Fin.

Ajit holds a master's degree in general management from Harvard University and a master's degree in computer information systems from the University of Phoenix. He also has a bachelor's degree in electrical engineering from India.

Ajit is passionate about sharing his knowledge and insights. He maintains a blog called "The Data World" (http://www.thedataworld.org), where he publishes articles, tutorials, and industry insights related to data, analytics, and emerging technologies.

With his extensive experience and technical skills, Ajit Dash continues to make significant contributions to the data and analytics field, empowering organizations to leverage the power of data for informed decision-making and strategic growth.

www.ingramcontent.com/pod-product-compliance
Lightning Source LLC
LaVergne TN
LVHW051615050326
832903LV00033B/4510